JASMINA BALOGH

The 30-Minute Entrepreneur

Build A Thriving Online Business in 30 Minutes a Day

First edition

This book was professionally typeset on Reedsy.
Find out more at reedsy.com

"The richest people in the world look for and build networks, everyone else looks for work."

ROBERT KIYOSAKI

Contents

1. Introduction   1

2. Network Marketing Is Not Your Cousin's Pyramid Scheme   5

3. Playful But Intentional Plan B   8

4. Crafting Your Vision and Goals   10

5. You Do Have 30 minutes a Day to Start Your Business!   13

6. The Pocket-Sized Power Packs a Punch   15

7. The Secret Sauce: Your Focus and Commitment   17

8. Thirty Minutes of Pure Productivity   20

9. Level Up You To Level Up Your Business!   25

10. Your Phone Is Your Friend   27

11. Overcoming Challenges, Staying Resilient   30

12. Scale Up and Out of This Book   32

1. Introduction

Welcome to this 30 minute Entrepreneur guide. I have been wanting to write it for years because so many people are not starting their business because they feel there is no time left in their day to do so, and I wanted to dispel that myth!

Others around you are starting businesses but you are uncomfortable and feel left behind. Maybe you don't know how or where to start on your journey to become an entrepreneur. You probably think that you just don't have the time to start a business in the middle of an already full family and business life, but I am here to tell you otherwise. 30 minutes a day is enough to get you going…. Forget all the excuses and just start! You can do it! I know because I did it many years ago!

You know how, when you think back, every single important step in our lives was a step into the unknown. It was a step that stretched us out of our comfort zone, just a bit further. When we finished elementary school, we were on top of the totem pole, only to enter middle school and be at the bottom again. After we finished middle school, we were the oldest kids at school, only to move to a brand new high school – at the bottom of the totem pole again. That's how life goes. It launches us from one step to another, up the stairway, in the direction of our own success, whether that's parenthood, career success, super fitness, art, music or entrepreneurship. Whatever rocks our boat the most!

First of all I want to congratulate you for picking up this book and deciding to start your own business or at least face some of your fears. This book will deal primarily with the fear of not having enough time or not knowing how to start your own home based/online business and it will not have all the answers but it will help you make the next step. After all - you only need to know where you are going, and what the next step is, and if you keep moving on, step by step, you are golden! Even when it seems that time, money, kids, parents, school, soccer games, government, weather, Covid, or whatever else you think is a justifiable and solid reason why you haven't started your business yet, this book will help you bridge that gap and make the next move.

I have to admit that I am just like you. It took me so long to start writing this book, because I just couldn't find the time to do it, so I am swallowing my own pill here. Guess what? I have even less time now, but I have become a better manager of my time, and I am able to accomplish so much more. Realize that you will Never have more time in your life than Now! (Stop reading and ponder this for a few moments!)

This book will introduce you to working from home, in an online network marketing industry, and also show you how you can start and build your business right from wherever you are, by working the business in 30 minute increments, in the nooks and crannies of your day. You Can start with literally 30 minutes a day, but you have to be committed. The key is your attitude, not the amount of time that you have!

Also, when I say that you can start - let's be clear that I did not say that you will finish and grow your business to a multi-million dollar business by working 30 minutes a day. Let's be realistic - most people take longer than that to eat every day. Nevertheless - 30 minutes a day will get you out of the gate and going in the right direction.

We are all familiar with the regular 9 to 5 jobs, and we don't even realize that we are sacrificing our life to our work. Our work takes the central part of our day and then we live our life around our work hours. That's your typical job situation. You spend 8 or more hours at work, and, to be perfectly honest, you don't even consider your productivity. You are doing what's expected of you, you are doing your best, someone is paying you for it, and that's it. If you are lucky, you have a flexible schedule, great coworkers, a nice office environment and your boss only cares that what needs to be done gets done.

If you are not lucky, your work environment is not so nice, your boss keeps switching your hours and micromanaging you, springing overtime in the last minute, and you're just not happy. You are trying to make the rest of your life work around your work hours, which is often very stressful, frustrating and hard. For most people, it is the reality of their life and they just don't see how to find the time, energy, money or motivation (or they think so), to look in the direction of their own business and freedom. For many, the world of entrepreneurship looks scary, daunting and risky. Isn't that what everything new and unknown, never seen or tried before, looks like anyway?

The goal of this book is to show you that everybody can start an online business, whether it's network marketing or some other type of online affiliate marketing, or something else that you can do remotely, online, from home. Even though we're going to focus on the network marketing businesses, the same principles will apply to all of the relationship marketing type businesses.

2. Network Marketing Is Not Your Cousin's Pyramid Scheme

I'm very much aware that network marketing is the phrase that makes uncle Bob cringe at family dinners, but let's set the record straight. I want to dispel the myths and reveal the golden pot of entrepreneurial potential that network marketing truly is.

I know that a lot of you have been brainwashed by older generations who have been involved in network marketing at its very beginnings, with companies that I will not mention by name. They were famous for filling up people's garages with products that they didn't need or could use as fast as they were required to purchase them in order to stay in business. Those practices, and most of those companies, are either gone, or they changed their business models because it simply didn't work. Unfortunately, this is what gave network marketing a bad name for years to come. Just like with everything else in life, online businesses, network marketing and relationship marketing businesses have evolved a lot in the last 15 to 20 years, and keep getting better and better.

A lot of companies that are coming to the market these days intentionally choose the network marketing distribution model because a lot of products that they market would just not sell in the regular storefront environment simply because no one would know their value. For example, if you walk into a store that sells vitamins and minerals, unless there is somebody there who can talk with you about the difference between all those bottles that look the same to layman's eye, you are simply going to buy whichever one is the cheapest, if you are a rational type. If you are an emotional buyer, you will most likely get the one that has the prettiest packaging, or the one that you have seen on TV or magazines you read. (Yes, we are all programmed. That is why it is called TV and radio programming.)

Let's focus back on our products... What if the product is so different from anything else, or maybe so small that it's practically invisible on the shelf, or maybe so cutting edge that somebody actually has to explain it to you before you're able to understand what it is and what it does, and how to use it correctly to get the most benefit from it. Do you think that somebody in your stores, supermarkets, mega chains or even local groceries is going to know or care enough about it, not to mention to take the time to do it. This is what makes the network marketing model unique. You don't just buy a random product. You are actually educated about the benefits of it by other customers who are using that product, people who are called associates, brand partners or distributors, and who have been educated by the company so that they can share with you the benefits of their product. That way, you can make an educated decision when buying it.

Those associates are independent contractors who get paid for educating customers and taking good care of them, and honestly - most of the time, they know a lot more and care a lot more than your everyday store employees who get paid the base hourly wage.

Just to address the pyramid scheme for those who are still stuck here.

Unlike legitimate business models, pyramid schemes do not create value through the sale of products or services. Instead, they redistribute funds from new recruits to those higher up in the pyramid, with the majority of participants inevitably losing money.

For something to be a pyramid scheme, there has to be an exchange of money with no product on the other side. In other words if you're purchasing a quality product, and you're getting it in exchange for your money, it is not a pyramid scheme.

It is important to note that pyramid schemes are illegal in most countries and will get shut down really fast, so if a network company has been around for 5,10,20 years - it is safe to assume it is legit!

If you think that network marketing companies are a pyramid scheme because of the way their distributors are paid, you need to know that their compensation is not very different from how big corporations pay their Presidents, VPs, regional directors, store managers and ultimately their basic employees. Doesn't that structure look like a true pyramid, and yet nobody is questioning it because we are just used to people on top making more than people at the bottom.

Once you truly understand network marketing compensation plans, you will realize that they are great equalizers of opportunities, and that those who work are paid the most, and even the newbies can move up the ranks, past the people who got into business long before them, and regardless of their race, nationality, creed, sex, beliefs or lifestyle.

3. Playful But Intentional Plan B

Network marketing has become really popular lately as a legitimate way of doing business. It's a way for people to make money by telling others about products they like. The cool thing is, you can keep earning money residually, for many years. This is called passive income which ultimately creates financial independence and it is a lot of fun to create and receive. The passive income comes from satisfied customers who keep using the product month after month because they love it, and this is one more reason why you have to choose your company wisely!

Network marketing leverages the power of personal connections and word-of-mouth marketing, allowing individuals to build their businesses by recommending products and services they genuinely believe in. With the right strategy and dedication, network marketers can create substantial income streams that continue to flow even when they're not actively working.

I am advocating for everyone to have a Plan B, in other words to start their own business, aside from what they're currently doing as their main job, even if it's just 30 minutes here and there, so about 3-5 hours a week. If you feel that you don't have that time, I will show you how to find it. You will definitely not be the first one to create additional cash flow outside of your 9-5 job!

Economic uncertainties and unforeseen circumstances, like Covid that hit us out of the blue, can impact any business, reinforcing the need for diversification. A plan B provides a safety net and an additional stability, ensuring that you and your family can adapt to changes while continuing to pursue your financial goals. In this dynamic landscape, embracing both the opportunities of network marketing, and the security of your job, it is a prudent approach to achieving lasting financial success.

I know you are all excited now so I have to add a warning: Do not leave your job until you're making, in your network marketing or other home-based business, at least as much as you have been bringing in through your regular job. If you spend some focused and dedicated time working on your business, and you are not in a hurry to leave your job, you really do not need many hours to get ahead. On the other hand, if you are tired of your job and can't wait to fire your boss, get away from your annoying coworkers, or simply want to retire and do something fun, start re-balancing your hours in favor of working from home and the balance will tip. And so will your checkbook!

So now that we are clear, and on the same page, let's talk about the most important thing in any business - your undivided Focus, even if it's just for 3 x 10 minutes a day.

4. Crafting Your Vision and Goals

There are multiple books written on the subject of how to craft your vision and your goals. I'm not going to go into details here but I just want to remind you that it is extremely important to have a big vision, and a big dream that you are walking towards, as well as long term and short term goals. Your dream should be so important and Big that it hovers in the forefront of your mind all the time!

What if I don't know what I want? What is my dream? I have been to busy with life in front of me. I had no time to dream! I have a few short-term goals but what is my vision - I don't know! If this is you - start from your goal. A simple one. Maybe you just want to make an additional $1,000 a month. You are most probably OK with this type of specific and practical goal. (This is just an example. Use a goal or a $ number that is true for you!) It should feel good to you, reasonable and achievable. Something that you can relate to. Don't write $30,000 a month if you believe that a $10,000 a month would be a huge stretch. Stretching is OK and healthy but keep it just outside of reach from where you are at the moment. When you get there, you will see further and set bigger goals! Think of climbing a mountain - the higher you go, the further you are able to see!

Here is a great exercise: Take a piece of paper and write down why you want this, or why does your goal matter. Then you ask why you want that, and keep going deeper and deeper. It should look something like this:

I just want an additional $1,000 a month.

Why?

Because it would make my family's life so much easier.

Why?

Because my husband and I would not have to fight over finances every month.

Why?

Because we would be able to pay all of our bills and maybe even save for a vacation?

Why does that matter?

We would feel like we have an upper hand on life.

Why does that matter?

Because we want to provide the best for our children and feel good about our life.

Why?

Because we are good people. We deserve it.

Why?

Because life feels much better when we can enjoy all that life has to offer….

There you go! In 7 simple questions, we went from wanting an additional $1,000 a month to the realization that we are worthy of enjoying our life and all it has to offer. We went 7 levels deep, and the deeper we let ourselves go, the closer we got to who we really are, and the more we felt how far we actually are from where we want to be. And that is painful. There is a saying that unless your Why makes you cry, it is not big enough! Your Big Why is very important because it will drive you forward and pull you out of the slump. It will keep you motivated and inspired, so take the time to do this process!

It is also important to write all that down because it gives you additional clarity while you are writing it and every time you see it in front of you. Make it big and put it on the wall where you see it every day! You want your goals to be SMART.

Specific
Measurable
Achievable
Relevant
Time-bound

Well-organized network marketing back office (all companies offer them, some for free and others at a charge) should help you design your goals and your vision, and follow your progress. You will be moving through the ranks and you will be increasing your income on a regular basis. This is where the team plays a huge role. In one and the same company there are different teams, and the team will often make you or break you by offering support and guidance, and by providing motivation and inspiration, versus a team that is not very active and not offering much to its members. Definitely something to consider!

5. You Do Have 30 minutes a Day to Start Your Business!

I know you don't believe me! I hear you loud and clear, so let's go over some things together! Let's crank up that time machine and let's first find you a sweet 30 minutes in your day to supercharge your business.

I don't know your specific timetable but here are 10 ideas to unearth those precious moments:

1. **Social Media Detox with a Twist:** Trim down your social media time by half. Suddenly, you're not just scrolling; you're becoming a business wizard. You are reaching out! Double win!
2. **TV Show Hustle:** Sacrifice one episode of your favorite show for focused business work. Trade entertainment for entrepreneurship – the coolest kind of trade-off.
3. **Lunch Break Power Hour:** Turn that hour into a power-packed business brainstorm. Salad and strategy – a combo for champions.
4. **Commute Commotion:** Utilize your commute for more than just glaring at tail lights. Podcasts, audiobooks, and voice notes are your new co-pilots to business success.
5. **Early Bird Entrepreneurship:** Wake up 30 minutes earlier to conquer your business to-dos. Who needs sleep when you're chasing dreams, right?

6. **Post-Kids Bedtime Blitz:** Once the kiddos are down for the night, it's your time to shine. Swap Netflix for business building, and watch your goals soar.

7. **Multitasking Masterclass:** Combine workouts with brainstorming sessions. Just imagine you're sweating out ideas along with calories. Put your earbuds in and learn more about your products. I call it an educational fitness session.

8. **Delegate and Elevate:** Delegate non-business tasks for 30 minutes. Your newly freed-up time? You guessed it – business bonanza.

9. **Technology Timeout:** Pause the endless notifications and emails for 30 minutes. Instead, tackle tasks that genuinely grow your business.

10. **Weekend Warrior Wisdom:** Carve out 30 minutes during the weekend for a concentrated business push. You're not just brunching; you're building an empire.

Choose any one of them, or even better, multiple ones, and start building your own empire in the nooks and crannies of your day! These 30-minute pockets are like mini time capsules packed with potential. Embrace them, conquer them, and watch your business dreams come to life. Time to hustle, time traveler!

6. The Pocket-Sized Power Packs a Punch

Guess what? Who says those 30 minutes have to be all together? Break them up however you see fit, just make sure your undivided focus is keeping you at task! Let's squeeze those minutes out of your day like you're trying to get the last drop of toothpaste from the tube. Here are 10 hilariously practical ideas to find those elusive 10 minutes for your business:

- **The Snooze Button Shuffle:** Trade hitting the snooze button for a mini brainstorming session or connecting with a friend in a different time zone. Who needs those extra zzz's when you can wake up with brilliant business ideas?
- **Elevator Pitchin' Potty Breaks:** Perfect your elevator pitch while perfecting your potty break. Multitasking at its finest – just make sure you're not in an actual elevator.
- **Traffic Jam Jamboree:** Stuck in traffic? Turn your car into a rolling business brainstorming HQ. Fellow commuters will wonder why you're grinning like a genius.
- **Microwave Mastermind Moments:** Waiting for your microwave burrito? That's a golden opportunity to quickly respond to your emails, tackle brief social media updates, or even read up on the latest industry trends.
- **Netflix Negotiation Breaks:** Netflix binges are cool, but imagine

the masterpiece you could craft during those "next episode starts in 10 seconds" moments while everyone else is fetching pop corn from the kitchen.

- **Lunch Break Lightning Round:** Instead of another cat video, use your lunch break to jot down ideas, connect with potential clients, or plan your next business move.
- **Phone Call Power Play:** Use those chit-chat calls with your pals to also check in with clients or follow up on your business leads.
- **Grocery Line Genius:** Instead of people-watching, whip out your phone and reply to those emails. The guy behind you in line might just be impressed by your business prowess.
- **Laundry Time Limelight:** Folding laundry doesn't have to be dull. Pop in some earbuds and listen to a business podcast or inspirational audio book. Laundry day - meet productivity day.
- **Waiting Room Wisdom:** Whether it's the doctor's office or the DMV, bring a notebook and work on your business to-do list. Suddenly, waiting doesn't feel so torturous.

Remember, finding those 10 minutes is like discovering hidden treasure – it might be disguised as mundane moments, but it's pure gold for your business dreams. So, go forth and conquer your 10-minute snippets of focused attention!

7. The Secret Sauce: Your Focus and Commitment

The central premise here is a laser-like focus on one's pursuits. If you divert your energies in too many directions, it will result in diffused, diluted outcomes. Whether you are a he, she or they, and whether you believe it or not - we humans are just not born multi-taskers! So, focus on the task ahead of you, and do first things first, and second things not at all! Eventually, as you accomplish your first things first, everything will fall in place in its natural order! This is definitely a great principle to take with you into all other areas of life.

The second principle that we'll use here is the Pareto Principle, also known as 80/20 rule. Picture yourself in a candy wonderland. You've got a magical candy bowl filled with all your favorite treats. Now, the "Pareto Principle" is like the candy fairy's spell that reveals an astonishing secret: 20% of those candies will give you a whopping 80% of your superpowers! Imagine munching on just a handful of candies – the chosen few – and suddenly you're invincible. That's the Pareto Principle in action. It's like the Universe's way of saying, "Hey, focus on the good stuff and watch the magic happen!"

Think of it as your personal treasure map to success. In a land of endless tasks and possibilities, the Pareto Principle whispers, "Psst, my friend, focus your energy on that glittering 20%, and the rest will fall into place." So, when you're lost in a forest of choices, just remember the Pareto Principle – your compass to navigating the candy wonderland of life. In the context of network marketing, this translates to a minority of your actions and efforts generating the majority of returns.

Decide what tasks belong to your A-list of Income producing activities and allocate all or most of your time to those super important tasks, and you will experience remarkable results. The key is to know what drives your business - things like...

- Creating potent relationships and connections that catalyze business growth,
- Talking to your customers or potential business partners,
- Educating them or showing them your products,
- Signing them up or helping them place their orders,
- Training your team, etc.

If you "religiously" allocate your efforts, this strategic approach can yield substantial dividends. Don't be fooled by other leisurely online activities like...

- Designing your business cards
- Creating the follow up system
- Organizing your office
- Writing lists of people you want to reach out to
- Choosing the type of calendar you want to use for business
- Arranging paper clips by color and shape
- Etc. Do you catch my drift?

These are definitely B-Z list activities related to your business. They may even be necessary and helpful, but they are not the top A-list ones that will effectively make your business grow.

The key to success is knowing the income producing activities in your own business and applying your focus in a very intentional, dedicated and consistent way to those activities, even if it's just 30 minutes a day, in between your other business or family obligations. Can you see how doing the right things will bring us the results we are looking for? Yay! This business is actually quite predictable. Don't you like that?

8. Thirty Minutes of Pure Productivity

OK, I get it! It's possible to work only 30 minutes a day and get my business going but what exactly am I supposed to do in that time period?

Since we're talking about the network marketing industry, it is easy to answer this question, and it doesn't matter what company you are with. Here are the 3 basic steps that will serve you well. This is all you need to work on. Those are the three key activities, your income producing activities, your key performance indicators, and when you master them - you become an unstoppable rock star!

#1. Put your products or services in front of the people who may have a need for them. Who are those people? Where do you find them? What do you tell them? I will give you some basic ideas here to get you started but your team leaders should train you and provide specific verbiage and advice.

In order to get your product in front of the people, your top priority is to reach out to at least 3 new people every day, the people that you have not talked about your product yet. Connect with them, create a relationship, and introduce them to whatever you have. The approach and the verbiage may differ from company to company and, leadership is a sign of a great team. Your leaders will provide the resources for you.

If you need help, talk to your leaders, and your up-team. If you feel like an orphan, and you are not getting any answers, guidance or support, reach out to me on LinkedIn. I may be able to help.

How do you execute this step? It can be done in many ways by reaching out to people in your phone contact app via calling or texting, by reaching out to people on social media, or by networking online and off-line.

Some people prefer to start from their warm market, which would be their friends and family members who they already have relationships with. If you have already been in the network marketing company (or a number of them), and you have blown your immediate contacts, so they don't want to hear about the next thing you are doing, skip them and start reaching out to people you don't know. You will be much better off! It will take a little bit longer, because you will have to establish those relationships first, but it will feel much better. Let your friends and family observe your success, and they will come back to you on their own, curious about what you are doing that's working so well for you.

The key, in this phase, is to reach out and truly create rapport, relationships, maybe even new friendships with like-minded people. Do not be pushy, and try to sell people on your products. Trying to even talk too much to your acquaintances about your products, during your first conversation, is just like asking someone to marry you on the first date. Not the best idea!

Nobody wants to be sold but everybody likes to be educated and have the information they need to make their own informed decisions. When asked, don't answer with a speech, especially not with a monologue!

People don't care how interesting and entertaining you are, nor how much you know. This is absolutely not about you. Respond briefly and ask more questions. Be curious and be interested. The answers you hear will let you know if this person can benefit from what you have.

Last but not least, use the tools that you have available – things like overviews, videos, white papers, testimonials, or whatever is appropriate in your business. Again, your team leaders will help you.

#2. Follow up with the people that you have already communicated with and see where they're at. They may or may not be ready to order your products. Make sure to answer their questions, provide more information if they need it, connect them with your team, or invite them to an event, online or off-line. Of course, you will be doing this only with people who are interested, ready and leaning forward. Do not try to drag or persuade people to do what you want them to do. People persuaded against their will are of the same opinion still!

Not everyone is your prospect, and not everyone needs or wants your products, no matter how great they are, and regardless of the fact that you think they are the best on the planet and that everyone needs them and should use them. Be courteous and polite to those who do not show interest. Always ask how you can help them and what you can do to help their family or business. Thank them for the time they spent with you and ask them if it's OK to touch base with them in 3-6 months, and/or send them a periodic email or text.

Life changes. New circumstances create new openings and opportunities. For the time being, leave them on the back burner and continue communicating with them periodically, as you would with your other friends and acquaintances. Comment on their posts, be a part of their lives, but don't mention business until a few months later, if you got permission to do so, and do it tastefully and non-intrusively. Again, despite what you think - not everyone will want your product, and that it OK!

#3 . Follow up and educate your customers, and help them better understand your products and business. At the same time, educate, lead and support your new and existing team members. Check in with them on a regular basis. Make sure you answer the questions that they have and guide them towards the resources. Invite them to team events, and company events, and make sure that you are attending those events so that you are informed and in the know about what's happening in your business. You want to be there for yourself and for your team.

So, if we look at the time structure of your day, if you have only one 30 minute segment a day to do your business or maybe you have three sets of 10 minutes on your brakes or while you're watching your kids sports activities, utilize that time effectively on those top 3 activities. It doesn't take long to reach out to 3 new people, check in with them, create rapport, and ask them about what's going on in their lives. If you establish that they have a need that your company can fulfill, product-wise or financially, by joining your team, that is the conversation that you will take to the next level.

Step 2 usually takes a little bit longer because you are either sharing information and resources, or inviting to events. Make sure you attend the events that you're inviting your friends and acquaintances to attend. They will feel much more comfortable seeing you there. You will also follow up right afterwards. If your schedule doesn't allow for that, ask your trainer/coach/sponsor to help you with it and they will happily do so. If you have never been in the network marketing business, you will very quickly realize that everybody up the team from you is very happy to help you. If they are not, you're either in the wrong company or on the wrong team.

As your team is growing, step 3 may require you to create more time on your schedule to dedicate to your business, or create a streamlined process that allows you to touch base with every member and customer at least once a month.

9. Level Up You To Level Up Your Business!

It may be very effective to use a 30 minute time to network online or in person. If you attend a networking event, especially the ones where you do a lot of one to one meetings, it is a great opportunity to meet 3-5 or even more people in a very short period of time.

The most important message of his chapter – Be gentle and patient with yourself. You will not be perfect from the beginning. You will suck, just like the rest of us did when we started, but don't let this take you down. There was a time that you totally sucked at reading and look at you now! Allow yourself to learn and grow!

Networking was a stretch for almost all of us but it is good to stretch your boundaries. Having your own business demands it. So, be ready for your demons to come out to haunt you - things like – "I don't know what I'm doing", "I just said something totally stupid","This person doesn't like me", "I look weird", "I just stuttered and chewed up my words", "I don't think I'm good at this", etc.

Guess what?! It's absolutely normal! We have all done it, and we made it. The more you do something the better you get. Do you know the song – What doesn't kill you makes you stronger! The more you push through, to the other side of fear, the more it is clear that this business is not a health hazard, that no one has died from public speaking, talking on Zoom, making a phone call, or sending an email. The more you grow as a person and a business owner - the more your business will grow. Newsflash!!! Have you noticed that those two things always go together? Your business will only grow as much as you do!

The best investment in an investment into yourself! Work on your personal development. There is a lot of free information available online and a lot of You Tube videos and courses that will help you become the best version of yourself! Great MLM teams and companies know this and invest in their people!

On my team, we often say that we are in a personal development company that also happens to have amazing products and a compensation plan attached to it. So, the sooner and more consistently you start doing those uncomfortable but necessary activities, the sooner you will become a pro! And a Pro Become You Will!

10. Your Phone Is Your Friend

If you are calling, texting or sending messages to reach out to your people, you can create templates that you can then copy and paste. It will drastically shorten your time. You will only continue communication with those who respond back to you. There are all kinds of software, apps and technology available to help you with this, but stay away from it all, at least at the beginning, because people don't like talking to bots, and you have to learn how to use them correctly.

In network marketing, different teams usually have different approaches so make sure to work with your leaders and follow their advice because there is a reason that they are leaders. They have already done what you are working on accomplishing, so don't be a smart aleck. Learn from them, do what they are doing, follow their advice and become their business clone.

Making phone calls can sometimes stir up common worries, like fearing rejection or stumbling over words. But fear not, there are solid strategies to conquer these concerns. First off, remember that every call is an opportunity, not a judgment. After creating rapport, kick things off, using conversation starters like, "I came across something that might interest you." Keep it casual and engaging. When they respond, focus on active listening. Pay attention to what they say, show genuine interest, and ask open-ended questions. Scripts can be super handy. For example, after a warm greeting, you could go with, "I noticed you're into [interest]. Have you ever thought about turning that passion into an income?" Remember, it's all about tailoring your talk to their world. Highlight how your offering can align with their unique goals and needs. By approaching calls/conversations with these strategies, you're not just overcoming doubts, you're creating genuine connections that pave the way for fruitful conversations.

Texting has emerged as a potent tool for communication within the realm of network marketing. Its convenience and immediacy make it an invaluable avenue to engage with prospects and team members alike. When crafting text messages, it's vital to strike a balance between being compelling and personalized. Start with a friendly greeting and reference something specific to their interests or previous interactions. This personal touch establishes a genuine connection. For instance, "Hey [Name], remember when we chatted about [topic]? I came across something I think you'd love." Additionally, ensure the value of your message is evident, whether it's a new opportunity or a product. However, while automation can streamline your efforts, don't forsake authenticity. Inject your unique voice and avoid robotic phrasing. Utilize automation selectively, perhaps for initial outreach, but pivot to personalized responses as the conversation evolves. Ultimately, successful texting in network marketing hinges on merging the efficiency of automation with the authenticity of personalization to build meaningful relationships that transcend the screen.

Keep in mind – some conversation can turn fruitful right away. Others are not quite ripe and need some patience, TLC and time to ripen. Of course, there are also those that never go anywhere. That's just how life is. You don't like every single person, nor do they like you, so don't take it to heart and just move on to the next person that you like and that likes you!

11. Overcoming Challenges, Staying Resilient

Network marketing, like any venture, comes with its fair share of challenges. Rejection and slow progress can test even the most determined individuals. However, these hurdles need not be roadblocks to success. Maintaining a positive mindset is the key. Embrace setbacks as learning opportunities, and remind yourself of your goals. Building resilience involves acknowledging that setbacks are a natural part of the journey. Seek support from mentors or peers, as they can offer insights and encouragement. Perseverance is crucial – progress might be slow, but every step counts. Take a breather when needed, and then return with renewed vigor.

When talking to people, there are 4 important rules that will help you overcome the challenges:

1. Emotionally detach from the outcome!
2. Be Yourself!
3. Bring some passion to the table!
4. Have a strong posture (even if you don't feel that confident). Be yourself, just your bolder self!

Stand in front of the mirror, and talk to yourself as if you are talking to your prospect, and have fun doing it! Make fun of yourself, intentionally. Make faces, show passion, grin, be ridiculous, talk back. Get used to looking at yourself in the mirror, being yourself. Practice! It may not make you perfect but it will certainly make you more comfortable, and not only when you are doing business. Day by day, you will start liking that person in the mirror more and more, and it will transfer into real life communications as relaxed confidence! Record a video, or two, maybe more! Not to send to anyone. Just to practice, to have fun and to get to know yourself. You will become a great communicator, networker, connector and educator.

My friend, let's call her May, faced multiple challenges and rejections before landing her breakthrough. She consistently reached out, adapted her approach, and kept refining her skills. Over time, her determination paid off, leading her to build a thriving network marketing business. Remember, success often hides behind challenges, waiting for those who persist despite the odds.

12. Scale Up and Out of This Book

The journey, from starting your side gig and establishing an initial network to scaling up and establishing a sustainable business model, marks a pivotal transition in network marketing. At this point, you will definitely be outside of the 30 min a day model. You may still be working in 30 minute increments, but to go full time, it is obvious that you have to dedicate a lot more than 30 minutes a day to your business. Think about your current job - how much can you expect to be paid for working only 30 min a day? The Pareto principle is still at work here but it is easy to see that, in order to scale your business up, you have to scale up the time you are devoting to it. As you are building your networking marketing business and income, and as it reaches and overtakes the current income from your job, it's time to move to the next level and graduate out of this book. You side gig is about to replace your current job and expand from there to new heights now that you are giving it all of your time and attention. Very exciting times!

While building the foundation is crucial, the true potential lies in expanding beyond personal efforts and beginning to leverage your time and efforts through the work and efforts of your team, and for that to happen, you need to work with your team. Mentoring and supporting team members becomes paramount. Cultivating a culture of collaboration and shared success propels the entire team forward.

This involves providing guidance, resources, and encouragement, empowering team members to develop their skills and lead effectively. The key ingredient is to stay in the mindset of a permanent student of life and business.

The landscape of network marketing is dynamic, and staying ahead requires adapting to industry trends and technological advancements. Evolution is the essence of growth, and an open-minded and humble approach to embracing change is pivotal in not only surviving but thriving in this industry. Through effective mentorship, a commitment to lifelong learning, and a collective spirit, the leap from individual success to a sustainable network of triumphs becomes an attainable reality.

Conclusion

I trust that the journey through this book has shed light on the transformative power of network marketing when approached with focused effort. We've explored the significance of targeted actions, the Pareto Principle's role in income-producing activities, and the art of meaningful conversations. Remember, success begins with as little as 30 minutes of dedicated work each day.

Now, it's your turn to take action. Don't wait! Start implementing the strategies discussed here. Reading this book will do as much for your business as looking at food will do for your hunger. It will wet your appetite. Unless you take action - you will never satisfy your desire. Commit to your path toward financial freedom and entrepreneurial success. Move your lifestyle gently from being "owned" by your boss to being self-managed and free. Become a work-from-wherever-I-am happy business owner. Take your business to the beach or camping. Work it around your family life. Write your own hours, take vacations when you want, and whenever you want. Create your own lifestyle! Your journey begins now – embrace it with enthusiasm and dedication.

I truly hope that you have enjoyed this book as much as I enjoyed writing it, and that you will find it useful as a motivation and inspiration to start your own business even if it seems that you have no time for one more thing in your life. It is important to get started on your side gig/plan B, and gain some momentum. It is always easier to move forward an object that is already in motion, and as that object keeps moving it gains more and more momentum. That is how side gigs turn into big businesses that take you from having a boss to being the boss!

If I can be of service, you can find me on LinkedIn.

May your business building days be filled with fun, joy and success!

P.S. If you found this book helpful, I would very much appreciate it if you left a favorable review for it on Amazon. It helps other people find it!

Appendix:

Below are just a few of my favorite resources for personal development, productivity and network marketing.

Abraham, Hicks, E., & Hicks, J. (2006). *The law of attraction: The Basics of the Teachings of Abraham.* Hay House, Inc.

Carruthers, B. (2015). *Building an empire: The Most Complete Blueprint to Building a Massive Network Marketing Business.*

Maxwell, J. C. (2007). *Failing forward: Turning Mistakes into Stepping Stones for Success.* HarperCollins Leadership.

Fogg, J. M. (1997). *The greatest networker in the world: The story that has changed the lives of millions Now it can change yours!* National Geographic Books.

Olson, J., & Mann, J. D. (2013). *The slight edge: Turning Simple Disciplines into Massive Success and Happiness.* Greenleaf Book Group.

Worre, E. (2013). *Go Pro: 7 Steps to Becoming a Network Marketing Profession*

Yarnell, M., & Yarnell, R. R. (2010). *Your first year in network marketing: Overcome Your Fears, Experience Success, and Achieve Your Dreams!* Crown.

Podcast - Gary Vaynerchuk. (2023b, August 23). Gary Vaynerchuk. https://garyvaynerchuk.com/podcast/

Feedspot. (2023, August 26). *FeedSpot for podcasters.* FeedSpot for Podcasters. https://podcasts.feedspot.com/network_marketing_podcasts/